Sports Illustrated
SOCCER

The Sports Illustrated Library

Sports Illustrated
SOCCER

By PHIL WOOSNAM
with PAUL GARDNER

Illustrations by
Russell Hoover

J. B. LIPPINCOTT COMPANY
Philadelphia and New York

U.S. Library of Congress Cataloging in Publication Data

Woosnam, Phil.
    Sports illustrated soccer.

    (Sports illustrated library)
    1. Soccer. I. Gardner, Paul, birth date II. Sports
illustrated (Chicago) III. Title.
GV943.W7   796.33'42   72-5629
ISBN-0-397-00908-9
ISBN-0-397-00909-7 (pbk.)

Cover and photographs on pages 16, 65, 78, 80, 92–93, 94:
Syndication International Ltd.

Photographs on pages 8 and 10: George Berger

Contents

Sports Illustrated
SOCCER

1
Soccer
in America

SOCCER'S popularity throughout the world is unmatched by any other sport. It is played by millions of men and boys in Brazil and Russia, Mexico and Israel, Sweden and Malaya, Iceland and Italy, and a hundred other countries from Albania to Zambia.

Yet there has always been this strange puzzle: just why has the United States resisted the call of soccer? The game was, after all, one of the first to be played here. The famous 1869 game between Princeton and Rutgers—which is claimed to be the start of intercollegiate football—was, in fact, clearly a soccer game. The rules were based on those drawn up in 1863 by the London Football Association—and in England the word "football" means soccer!

The origins of soccer have been variously traced back to ancient Rome or Greece or Egypt or China. No one really knows where it all started—recreation involving kicking and chasing a round object seems always to have been a part of man's life. But it is that 1863 date which is held to mark

9

the birth of the modern game. When the London Football Association published its rules, it gave soccer its official title: Association Football. The word soccer is believed to be derived from Association, first shortened to Assoc., then corrupted to Soccer.

The game developed rapidly in England—a professional league was operating by 1888—and was carried all over the world by English sailors and settlers. Almost everywhere it was enthusiastically taken up by the local inhabitants, who were soon adding touches and refinements of their own. Over the years these differences in approach to soccer have developed into distinct national styles. There is today a Brazilian style, an English, a Hungarian and an Italian style and so on.

But while this world of international sports friendship was developing, while the names of soccer's great stars were becoming a common language amongst fans everywhere, the United States went its own way, with its own sports, baseball and football.

Certainly, there was soccer in the United States, but apart from its popularity in the Ivy League colleges, it was played almost exclusively by recently arrived immigrants.

And for nearly a hundred years soccer remained an immigrant sport. Until the late 1960s, when the soccer explosion began. Interest in the game had been growing steadily but now there was a dramatic jump in the number of colleges and high schools playing it. At last, soccer was becoming an American sport, played by American boys. The establishment of a professional league at about the same time completed the familiar pattern of the other American sports: youth program—high school—college—pros. The first draft of college players was held in 1972, opening up the possibility of a new career for young American athletes: pro soccer.

11

Diagram 1. The Soccer Field

Dimensions are permitted to vary within the following limits:

> Length: not more than 130 yards, not less than 100 yards.
> Width: not more than 100 yards, not less than 50 yards.
> (The length must always be greater than the width.)

Other dimensions remain fixed, whatever the size of the field:

> Goal area: 20 yards wide by 6 yards deep.
> Penalty area: 44 yards wide by 18 yards deep. (The goal area is part of the penalty area.)
> Penalty spot: 12 yards from the goal line.
> Penalty arc: radius of 10 yards about the penalty spot.
> Goal: 8 yards wide by 8 feet high.
> Center circle: radius of 10 yards about the center spot.
> Corner area: 1 yard in radius.

Flags **must** be placed at the corners of the field, but are optional at the halfway-line positions.

> (Scale of field shown: 110 yards by 80 yards.)

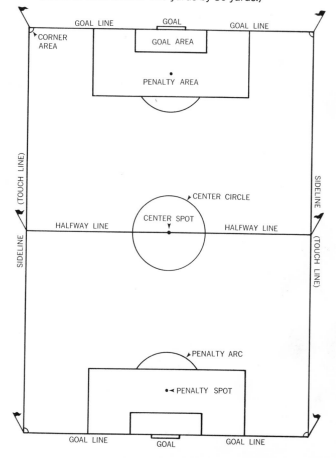

2
The Game

SOCCER is a game of continuous action and constantly changing possession, something like a cross between hockey and basketball, a team game in which each player is nevertheless clearly an individual with a style and skills all his own. Watching soccer games presents no problem because the rules (with the possible exception of the offside rule) are straightforward and easy to follow.

Each team has eleven players who try to get the ball into their opponents' goal. The full-size ball measures between 27 and 28 inches in circumference (an inch less than a basketball), but a smaller 24-inch ball is available for boys of ten years and under. One member of each team, the goalkeeper, guards the 8-yard-by-8-foot goal, and he is allowed to use his hands within his own penalty area (see Diagram 1). The other ten players are not allowed to use their hands at all. Players' equipment consists of shirt, shorts and socks and either soccer shoes (which have small round studs on the sole and heel) or sneakers. Some players use shin guards inside their socks, and some goalkeepers wear gloves.

The game is normally played in two 45-minute halves, with a 5-to-10-minute interval; but shorter periods, e.g. 30-minute halves, are recommended for younger players. Play is controlled by a single referee assisted by two linesmen, or, in college and high school games, by two referees.

The players control and move the ball with their feet, their legs, their head—in fact almost any part of the body except the hands and arms. If during play the ball goes over the sideline and was last played by a member of Team A, it is put back into play by a *throw-in* (see page 50) taken by a member of Team B. Here the hands *are* used, but the player is standing outside the field of play when he makes the throw.

If the ball goes over the goal line (other than into the goal) and was last played by the attacking team, it is put back into play with a *goal kick*; the ball is placed within the goal area and kicked upfield by a member of the defending team (often, but not always, the goalkeeper). If the ball was last played by a member of the team defending that goal line, it is put into play with a *corner kick* taken by the attacking team from the corner area.

There are nine major fouls in soccer. Four of them involve use of the hands: the obvious one—handling the ball *—plus holding, pushing or striking an opponent. Two involve use of the body: charging an opponent violently or dangerously, and charging from behind—though one form of body contact, the shoulder charge, is permitted (see page 66). Three involve use of the feet: tripping, kicking or jumping at an opponent. After any of these fouls the referee will award a *direct free kick*, to be taken at the point where the foul occurred, against the offending team, whose players must back off at least 10 yards from the ball. The kicker can score a goal directly from such a kick.

* Note that handling the ball covers both hands and arms, and is limited to *intentional* handling.

If one of the nine major fouls is committed by the defending team in its own penalty area, the attacking team is awarded a *penalty kick*. The ball is placed on the penalty spot, and a player of the attacking team takes a shot at goal with only the goalkeeper to beat; all the other players, of both teams, must be outside the penalty area and penalty arc. The goalkeeper is not allowed to move his feet until the ball has been kicked. In top-class soccer, failure to score on a penalty kick is rare.

There are a number of minor offenses—e.g., obstructing an opponent, arguing with the referee—which are penalized with an *indirect free kick* against the offending team. Here, the kicker cannot score a goal direct—he must kick the ball to another player first.

Among the offenses for which an indirect free kick is awarded is *offside*—and this is the one soccer rule that may at first be difficult to grasp. Briefly, an attacking player is offside if, at the moment the ball is passed to him, he

(1) is ahead of the ball—i.e., nearer to his opponents' goal line, *and*

(2) has fewer than two opponents between him and the goal line, *and*

(3) is in his opponents' half of the field.

The difficulties of the offside rule arise from the fact that it is not the player's position when he gets the ball that matters—it is where he *was* when the pass to him was made. A player cannot be offside if he receives the ball from an opponent or direct from a goal kick, corner kick or throw-in.

We have presented here a summary of soccer's most important rules. For fuller details you should consult the official rules of the game.

3
Ball Skills

LEARNING the soccer rules outlined in the preceding chapter will enable you to watch games with a full understanding of what is going on. But in learning the fundamental skills of soccer, you need really know only one rule: don't use your hands.

This is the rule that makes soccer unique among team sports. It means that you have to learn to control the ball —that round, lively, bouncey, slippery, elusive ball—without using your hands. You have to be able to make it do whatever you want—but only by using your feet, your legs, your body or your head. That is the basic challenge in learning soccer. Before you can think about mastering opponents, you must learn to master the ball.

Nobody is born with these skills. They can be learned and perfected only by hours and hours of devoted individual practice. And they are best learned away from the competitive pressures of actual games. All that is needed is a ball, a wall—and you. That is all. You do not have to be exceptionally tall or exceptionally muscular to play soccer. Most of the great soccer players are of average build. Their greatness comes, not from size, but from skill.

While you are learning and practicing the skills described below, remember these points:

• Soccer is a game of almost continual movement, one that calls for players to be alert at all times, to be ready to move quickly in any direction. Try to keep on your toes as much as possible, with your body relaxed and loose and your knees slightly bent.

• Keep your eye on the ball at all times.

• Balance is particularly important in soccer, where you are using your feet not only for running but for playing the ball. Learn to use your arms to maintain perfect balance.

• Practice with both feet. Although you are naturally either left- or right-footed, make sure that your other foot gets at least half the work in all the skills. To be a good soccer player, you must be able to use both feet.

• Most of the skills described here can also be practiced with a small ball such as a tennis ball. This can be extremely helpful in perfecting technique, particularly timing and touch, and a small ball can be carried around in your pocket, allowing you to practice whenever you have the opportunity.

GETTING USED TO THE BALL

First of all, here are two exercises designed to accustom you to the feel of the ball at your feet, to start the process by which playing the ball with the feet becomes natural to you:

Ball Control Exercise—1. Stand on your toes, your feet about 12 to 18 inches apart, and jump lightly from foot to foot. Raise your feet only about 3 inches above the ground and swing the legs from side to side, *not* backward and forward. Practice this briefly without the ball until you are used to the motion. Repeat the exercise with the ball between your feet, tapping it smoothly to and fro from foot to foot and keeping it on the ground. Learn to vary the speed

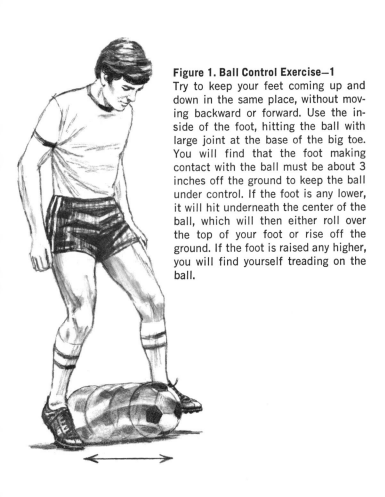

Figure 1. Ball Control Exercise—1
Try to keep your feet coming up and down in the same place, without moving backward or forward. Use the inside of the foot, hitting the ball with large joint at the base of the big toe. You will find that the foot making contact with the ball must be about 3 inches off the ground to keep the ball under control. If the foot is any lower, it will hit underneath the center of the ball, which will then either roll over the top of your foot or rise off the ground. If the foot is raised any higher, you will find yourself treading on the ball.

at which you perform the exercise, changing smoothly from fast to slow rhythms and back again to fast. At all speeds the touch of your foot on the ball must be just right: too hard, and the ball will get away from you, too light and you will not be able to maintain your rhythm.

Ball Control Exercise—2. In the previous exercise the idea was to keep the ball in motion on the ground; here, it is to keep the ball in motion *off* the ground by kicking or tapping it lightly up in the air in front of you. Your first attempts will probably send the ball spinning off in all directions, so that you will have to do a fair amount of running about to keep it from touching the ground. But as your control improves, it should be possible to keep the ball airborne while standing in one spot.

You can start the exercise by allowing the ball to bounce in front of you, but you should learn the knack of flicking a ground ball up in the air with your foot. Place the ball on the ground about 12 or 18 inches in front of you and rest the sole of your foot lightly on it. Draw your foot slowly

Figure 2. Ball Control Exercise—2
Use the area on top of your foot—where the instep ends and toes begin—to hit the ball, which you should try to keep going up and down between waist and knee height, about 12 inches in front of you. Vary the speed of your juggling, first bouncing the ball quickly by keeping it low, then slowing the rhythm by tapping the ball higher up to waist level. Practice with both feet—the ideal is to use each foot alternately.

backward, causing the ball to roll toward you. As soon as it starts moving, take your foot away and place it on the ground alongside your standing foot so that the ball rolls up over the toe. As soon as that happens, bend your toe upward and at the same time lift your foot off the ground. This will flick the ball straight up in the air, and you can carry on with the exercise.

KICKING

So-called "soccer-style" kicking, with its angled approach to the ball, has been much in the news in recent years due to the success that players such as Garo Yepremian, Jan Stenerud and Pete Gogolak have enjoyed in professional football. Actually, these field-goal kickers are using only one of several different types of kicks that a soccer player must master.

When first introduced to soccer, young players throughout the world tend to kick with their toes. In the initial stages this is certainly the easiest method of producing power and distance with your kick; but you will soon realize, especially when playing under wet conditions, that accuracy and delicate touch are virtually impossible to achieve with the toes. The earlier you practice the recognized soccer kicks described in this section, the sooner you will become an accomplished player.

Practice all the various styles of kicks described by kicking the ball against a wall. But do not start out by trying to knock the wall down—concentrate instead on acquiring a smooth action. The Golden Rules of kicking are:

● Approach the ball with a regular striding run—no hurried steps.

● Be sure to place your standing foot in precisely the right spot.

● Concentrate on a rhythmic swing of the leg, and on making contact with the correct part of the foot.

Inside-of-the-Foot Kick. Whenever accuracy is more important than power or distance, use this type of kick. The majority of passes of up to 20 or 25 yards are made in this manner, and, with practice, it is surprising how hard a side-foot pass can be hit. The twist of the hip, knee and ankle required to produce the correct angle for the foot may at first seem a little unnatural, but persevere, and you will soon get used to it.

Figure 3. Inside-of-the-Foot Kick
A. Place your standing foot alongside the ball at a distance of about 6 inches. Strike the center of the ball with the solid part of the foot indicated in 3B. The kicking foot should be about 2 inches off the ground as the kick is made.
B. The center of contact is marked 0.
C. Do not stop the kicking motion as soon as your foot hits the ball, but allow your leg to swing forward for another 12 inches or so. Be sure to keep your head down, watching the ball throughout the kick.

Instep Kick. This is the "soccer-style" kick, in which the instep—the flat top part of your foot where the shoe is laced—is used to strike the ball. There are two basic versions: the lofted kick and the low drive. With both types, the technique will vary slightly from player to player, according to foot size. Young boys, and others with small feet (size 8 and below), will be able to make these kicks with the toes of the kicking foot pointing straight down. But for most players such a position would result either in the toes stubbing the ground or the ball being hit too low on the instep. They must therefore turn their toes slightly outward.

The aim is to use the part of the instep shown in the illustrations as the center of contact, and to use the curve of the ankle joint to literally "wrap" itself around the curve of the ball. What happens immediately after impact—before the ball has started to move—is shown in Figure 4C.

Figure 4. Instep Kick
A. Small-footed players can point their foot straight down and kick the ball with the full instep. The center of contact is marked 0.
B. Most players, however, will have to turn their foot slightly outward and kick with the inside part of the instep—the center of contact is marked 0.
C. On impact, the foot sinks into the ball so that a large surface area of the foot meets a large surface area of the ball. This is what gives the instep kick its power and allows the player to control its direction.

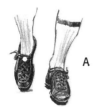

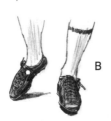

The Lofted Kick. This is the long-distance kick, and the kicking motion is designed to lift the ball high into the air. For this reason the point of contact on the ball is slightly *below* the center line, i.e., slightly underneath the ball.

Figure 5. Lofted Kick

A. Approach the ball from a slight angle —from the right if you are kicking with your left foot. Place the standing foot 6 to 9 inches to the side of—and slightly **behind**—the ball. Allow the kicking leg a full backswing, with the knee almost fully bent.

B. At the moment of contact, lean your body backward so that—

C.—your foot is beginning to swing upward as it strikes slightly below the center line of the ball.

D. Kick right through the ball, allowing the leg to swing into a full follow-through, with the toes pointing in the direction of the flight of the ball.

B

C

D

Figure 6. Low Drive

A

A. To keep the flight of the ball low, place the standing foot alongside, rather than behind, the ball, and lean your body forward so that—

B.—at the moment of impact the knee of the kicking foot is directly over—or even slightly in front of—the ball. Contact is made with the center of the ball so that the toes are pointed more sharply downward (C) than for the lofted kick. Straighten your knee powerfully as the kick is made, and make a full follow-through.

D. The front view of the low drive shows how the thigh and knee of your kicking foot should be pointing at the ball. Note the full use of arms to maintain perfect balance.

The Low Drive. The low drive is the kick that scores goals. Hard, accurate shooting at goal can only be achieved by mastering this kick.

Chipping. When an opponent is positioned to intercept the normal side-foot pass, your best alternative is to chip the ball over his head. The aim in chipping is to make the ball rise *steeply* into the air—it should clear an opponent who may be standing only 6 yards away. It is not a powerful kick, and the ball should not rise too high in the air—10 feet off the ground is ample. Start your practice with the ball rolling toward you—this is the easiest type of ball to chip. Use an action similar to the lofted instep kick in Figure 5B, page 25, but this time do not point your toes down. Instead, keep the heel down so that the foot is horizontal and just clipping the ground when the ball is struck. Your foot will hit the underside of the ball, and at the moment of contact, bend the toes upward, lean the body backward and use the inside of the instep to scoop the ball up. Your foot should slide under the ball, tending to give it backspin as it rises into the air. There is not a great deal of thigh movement in the chip kick; the leg swing is almost entirely from the knee, and it must be a decisive downward swing followed by a slightly lazy upward follow-through.

It is far more difficult to chip a stationary ball, and extremely difficult to chip one moving away from you. A more pronounced scooping action is necessary and also a greater follow-through. You should also practice rolling a stationary ball slightly backward or even sideways, using the sole of the foot (as described on page 20) before making the chip shot.

Outside-of-the-Foot Kick. While kicks made with the outside of the foot are lacking in power, they are extremely useful for quick and deceptive passing, because the ball can be flicked away at the last moment of what looks like a normal running stride.

As a variation, instead of kicking through the center of the ball and following through along the direction that the

Figure 7. Outside-of-the-Foot Kick
Turn the toes of your kicking foot inward and aim the marked part of the foot at the center of the ball.

ball travels, swing your leg slightly across the ball, hitting it off center with the outside of your foot. This will impart a spin that will cause the ball to swerve in flight.

RECEIVING

All the kicks so far described began with the ball stationary on the ground. When you first start to practice them against a wall, you will make more rapid progress if you do not attempt to kick the moving ball as it bounces back to you. Stopping it and setting it up for another dead-ball kick will allow you to control your kicks more carefully, and will also allow you to learn another of soccer's essential skills: receiving, or bringing a moving ball under control.

In game situations the ball will occasionally come to you exactly where you want it, the result of a perfect pass from a teammate. But far more often it will arrive less perfectly: perhaps too high or traveling too fast or to the wrong side of you. No matter—wherever or however it turns up, you must be able to control it at once with any part of your body, except your hands and arms of course. Usually the object is to get the ball at your feet as quickly as possible so that you are ready to dribble it forward, make a pass or take a shot at goal.

Controlling Ground Balls. In trying to stop a hard-hit ball coming back at you off the wall, you will quickly discover that merely sticking out a foot is not good enough. The ball hits the foot and bounces away again. To prevent this,

Figure 8. Controlling Ground Balls

A. Position yourself at an angle of about 45° to the path of the ball. Lift the controlling foot off the ground as the ball approaches, then lower it and move it backward at the same time.

B. After contact, the controlling foot continues to move backward, slowing the ball down until it can be stopped about 2–3 inches behind the point of original contact. The foot should be about 3 inches off the ground when contact is made with the ball. Any higher and a fast-moving ball may skid underneath; any lower and the ball may roll over the top.

you must develop the art of cushioning the ball, of making that area of your body meeting the ball "give" slightly as contact is made. Figure 8 illustrates the technique for controlling a ball coming fast along the ground.

Receiving and Turning. Vary this technique by facing the oncoming ball and, instead of stopping it, changing its direction by tapping it lightly with the inside of your foot so that it passes behind your standing leg.

Figure 9. Receiving and Turning—1
Immediately you have redirected the ball with your right foot, pivot on your left foot and run after the ball, keeping it within easily playable reach.

31

As another exercise in receiving and turning, practice the feint and full pivot shown in Figure 10. Remember, quickness off the mark, particularly when turning, is a tremendous asset. Get into the habit of making last-second deceptive moves, but be sure that you keep the ball within reach and that you move off smartly after the feint.

Figure 10. Receiving and Turning—2

A. As ball approaches, lunge forward and leftward with your left foot, as though about to gather the ball with the inside of your right foot and turn left, or to make a pass with your right foot.

A

C. Pivot on your right foot, moving off quickly after the ball and keeping it under close control.

B. Instead, allow the ball to roll until you can meet it with the **outside** of your right foot, taking most of the pace off it and allowing it to roll slowly to the right as you move your weight back to your right foot.

33

Trapping. So now you can control, and redirect, a ball rolling toward you along the ground. But most of those balls coming back off the wall will be in the air. Bringing them under control is known as trapping the ball. The following illustrations show the six most commonly used traps. For all of them, the key rule is: Do not stand still, flatfooted, waiting for the ball to come to you. Keep on your toes and adjust your position and body angle to the ball so that you can control it with confidence.

Figure 11. Inside-of-the-Foot Trap

Place your standing foot slightly ahead of where you anticipate the ball will bounce. The trapping foot should be about 6 inches off the ground and the ball is met at the moment it strikes the ground. The foot and the lower part of the leg must be leaned slightly over the top of the ball, and must be relaxed enough to smother the upward bounce. Do not jab at the ball or you will almost certainly cause it to bounce away.

Figure 12. Sole Trap

If the ball is falling too rapidly for you to get into position to trap it with the inside of your foot, stretch your leg forward and trap the ball in front of you, using the sole of your foot. Trap the ball as it hits the ground and, using a relaxed ankle joint, stifle the bounce with the sole of the foot.

Figure 13. Outside-of-the-Foot Trap

Apply the same principles as in the two previous traps: Meet the ball as it hits the ground, lean the foot and lower leg over it to smother the bounce.

Your aim should be to develop your trapping skill to the point where you can not only take the pace off the ball in one delicate action but also direct it to the exact spot on the ground for you to perform your next move.

Figure 14. Thigh Trap

A dropping ball coming at you at just below waist height is best dealt with by using a thigh trap. Raise your leg, with the knee bent, and allow the ball to make contact with the soft fleshy inside part of the thigh. To obtain the cushioning effect, lower the thigh slightly while relaxing the muscles at the precise moment of impact, so that the ball rebounds an inch or two before dropping to your feet.

Figure 15. Chest Trap—1
To control a ball at chest height, the vital consideration is the direction of the ball's approach. If the ball is dropping, lean back so that your chest forms a platform on which the ball lands. On impact, relax and withdraw the chest slightly to cushion the ball so that it bounces only 3 or 4 inches upward before dropping to your feet.

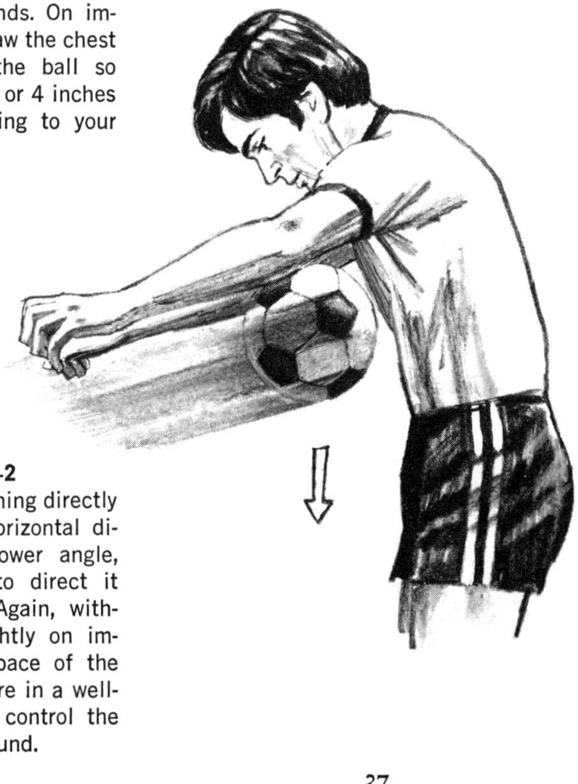

Figure 16. Chest Trap—2
For a hard-hit ball coming directly at your chest in a horizontal direction or from a lower angle, lean over the ball to direct it down to your feet. Again, withdraw your chest slightly on impact to reduce the pace of the ball. Make sure you are in a well-balanced position to control the ball as it hits the ground.

37

HEADING

"But doesn't it hurt?" That is always the thought of anyone asked to head a ball for the first time. The answer is: No, it does not, *if you do it correctly*. You must make sure that you use the center of the forehead—not the top nor the side of the head.

To dispel any doubts you may have about heading, hold the ball about 6 inches in front of your face and bounce it off your forehead, catching it as it returns and keeping your eyes open and your head still. Gradually increase the distance of the ball until you are holding it as arm's length. By this time you should be able to bounce it quite hard off your forehead without being afraid of it. It is simply a question of confidence.

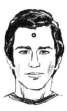

Figure 17. Heading
Use the center of the forehead to head the ball.

Ball Control Exercise—3. Familiarize yourself with the skill by using your head to keep the ball airborne, trying not to send it more than 12 or 18 inches above your head. Combine this exercise with Exercise—2, page 20: If the ball drops too low for you to head it, play it with your feet to keep it from touching the ground, then kick it just high enough for you to head it again. Keeping it airborne is a sure sign that you have developed a good sense of touch and ball control.

Figure 18. Ball Control Exercise—3
Keep your head bent well back and keep on your toes in order to maintain your position directly under the ball.

Basic Heading Technique. Power and distance in heading are achieved by getting as much of the weight of your body behind the ball as possible, and by perfect timing. *Go after the ball*—it is as though you are punching it with your forehead. Keep your eyes open all the time (though they will probably blink for a fraction of a second at the moment of impact) and hit the ball decisively with your forehead, rather than let it hit you.

Figure 19. Heading

A. Keeping your eyes fixed on the approaching ball, bend your body backward at the waist.

B. Swing the whole top half of your body forward, using your neck muscles to thrust your forehead at the ball so that you head it decisively downward.

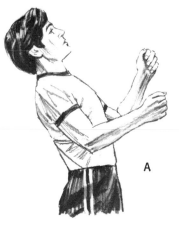

A

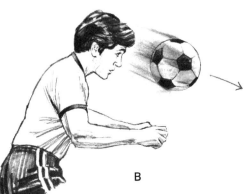

B

Jumping to Head the Ball. In games you won't often have the luxury of heading the ball with both feet on the ground. Usually you will have to jump for it, jackknifing in mid-air to produce the swing of the body that is required.

Learn to time your jump so that you are at maximum

40

height a fraction of a second before the ball arrives. Jumping too late is the most common fault in heading.

The ultimate, supreme skill—and what a graceful, exciting sight it is—is to soar into the air, apparently hover for a moment, then explode to flash the ball wide of a groping goalkeeper.

Figure 20. Jumping to Head the Ball
A. Jump sufficiently early so that you are an inch or two higher than the ball just before contact. Kicking your legs up behind you will help you to arch your back, so that—
B.—you can jackknife your body, throwing your forehead at the ball and directing it powerfully downward.

41

VOLLEYING

As you increase your skill at the types of kicks so far discussed, you will be able to speed up your off-the-wall practice by playing the moving ball straight back without stopping it. The kicking techniques are exactly the same as for a stationary ball—but, of course, your timing must be extremely accurate. In particular, because both you and the ball are moving, you must learn to judge as early as possible where to position your standing foot. If you do not get into the correct position before the ball arrives, your kick is almost certain to be inaccurate.

Under playing conditions probably about half the balls will come to you above ground level. To be able to play them first time, on the volley, without controlling them first —and to make them go where you want them to go!—is one of the most satisfying, *and* the most difficult, skills to master.

Side-foot Volley. This is used for balls coming at you between ankle and just above knee height. As with inside-

Figure 21. Side-foot Volley
Raise your leg with the thigh horizontal or pointing upward—depending on the height of the ball to be played—and with the foot turned outward. Meet the ball with a short, firm, forward swing of the foot—6 to 9 inches is all that is needed. The angle of your leg and foot on impact will govern the height of the pass you make.

of-the-foot kicking, you are aiming for accuracy and control rather than power and distance.

The reverse action is used to control the ball: on contact, *draw the foot back* slightly, perhaps 2 to 3 inches, so that the ball drops lightly to the ground. Without doubt, side-foot volleying and ball control are two of the most important skills to perfect.

Instep Volley: Low Balls. Volleying with power and for distance requires a different technique. You must point

Figure 22. Instep Volley: Low Balls

Keep your toes pointed down and kick with a sharp knee movement without making too great a follow-through. Keep your body and head leaning forward.

your toes down and hit the ball with the full instep. To keep the ball low—when shooting at goal for instance—get your body and your knee over the ball but do *not* make an enormous swing of the leg at the ball. To slash at it as though you are trying to kick it through the wall will make correct timing almost impossible—and it is perfect timing that is the secret of powerful volleying.

Practice by bouncing the ball in front of you, making a two-stride approach and volleying the dropping ball when it is 6 to 12 inches off the ground. Try to keep its flight below a height of 5 feet. When your timing has been perfected, gradually increase the power of your swing through the final 6 inches before impact. It is a beautiful sensation to crash the ball against the wall on the volley, while keeping it at a constant height of about 12 inches. You immediately have a vision of a goalkeeper hopelessly beaten as the ball flashes into the net.

Instep Volley: High Balls. If the ball arrives at or just above knee height, it is impossible to use the same frontal technique. You cannot get your knee over it, and all you will do is loft it high into the air. Figure 23 shows you one way of dealing with this situation.

Figure 23. Instep Volley: High Balls

Turn your body at an angle to the ball and swing your kicking leg almost horizontally. Again, a great scything swing of the leg is not necessary—just make a short firm jab from the knee, using the full instep to kick the ball. As your body will be leaning away from the ball, spread your arms wide to maintain your balance.

Instep Volley: Defensive Clearance. Defenders use defensive volleying to clear the ball away first time from the goal mouth, and the aim is to kick for distance.

Figure 24. Instep Volley: Defensive Clearance

A

B

A. As the ball comes in, firmly plant your standing foot and swing your kicking leg from the thigh.

B. Kick the ball at about knee height—but note that the knee is **not** over the ball. Kick with the full instep.

C. Lean your body backward as the kick is made, spreading your arms wide for balance.

D. Make a full follow-through, rising up on the toes of the standing foot.

Half-Volley. When you can't quite get to the ball before it hits the ground, you may be able to half-volley it by kicking it immediately after it bounces. Allow it to bounce no more than an inch upward before you kick it. When shooting at goal, the technique is the same as for the low instep volley: Place your standing foot level with or slightly in front of the ball, kick from the knee using the full instep and keep your knee over the ball. As the ball is already moving upward, if you are even fractionally late in kicking it you will tend to kick it high in the air. This is good for a defender trying to clear, but not for a forward shooting at goal. To pass the ball on the half-volley, where accuracy rather than power is required, use the inside or the outside of the foot.

Overhead Volley. To volley the ball behind you is not difficult as long as you can lift it in an arc over your own head. The ball is hit at about waist level or a little higher, and the position is similar to that in Figure 24D, page 47, except that the toes, instead of being pointed out, are pulled back, making the ankle joint into a right angle that directs the ball backward.

But to volley a ball backward—*and keep it low*—is something that even top-class players find difficult. The problem is to get the top part of your body out of the path of the ball—and this can be done only by falling backward as you throw your legs up into the air to kick the ball.

You will, inevitably, land on your back after the kick, and it is the fear of a painful landing that prevents many players from successfully making this kick. To gain confidence, practice falling backward while throwing your legs up in the air and using the hands to break your fall. You should land on your back, just below the shoulder level. Repeat the action with the ball, throwing it just above head height and about a foot in front of you, completing the action as in Figure 25B. In games, this is a kick that must be used with caution. High kicking, when other players are nearby, is a dangerous-play offense.

48

Figure 25. Overhead Volley

A. Swing the kicking foot off the ground first, followed by the nonkicking foot, while allowing the top half of your body to fall backward.

B. Hit the ball at about shoulder height with a sharp knee action, and with the toes pressed back toward your shin. Note the position of the hands, palms down, ready to break the player's fall.

THE THROW-IN

An oddity among soccer skills because it involves use of the hands, the throw-in is sometimes neglected, being viewed merely as a method of getting the ball back into play rather than as a dangerous attacking skill. Although you are not allowed to score by throwing the ball into the goal, a long throw can put the ball directly into your opponents' goal area to set up chances for others to score. The method of taking a throw-in, as laid down in the rules, is shown in Figure 26. If you make the throw incorrectly—a foul throw —you are not given a second chance. The ball goes over to the opposing team to throw in.

Figure 26. Throw-in
The throw-in must be executed with **both** hands on the ball (it is illegal to favor one hand) and must be delivered from behind and over the head. Some part of both feet must be on the ground, either on or outside the touchline. Spread your fingers out wide and position your hands so that the thumbs almost meet at the back of the ball, as shown in 26B. Some players take a one- or two-step run-up before throwing the ball, but most of the power in a throw-in comes from combining vigorous arm and wrist action with a strong swing of the body from the waist.

B

A

DRIBBLING

Dribbling, as in basketball, is the skill of beating opponents by keeping the ball under close control, while making deceptive changes in direction and pace. Making fairly short

Figure 27. Dribbling
A. Dribbling with the inside of the foot.
B. Dribbling with the outside of the foot.
C. This is the method of kicking the ball when dribbling with the **outside** of the foot. The foot is swung forward and turned as soon as it has made contact with the ball, so that you land on your toes in a normal running position.

strides, you keep pushing the ball along with the inside and the outside of your feet, making sure that the kicking foot is raised an inch or two from the ground to make a solid contact with the ball.

Note that the parts of the foot used are not quite the same as those used in kicking. It is the inside and outside of the *front* part of the foot, nearer to the toes, that do the dribbling. These areas allow a more sensitive touch that enables you to tell exactly how far ahead to push the ball so that you can play it in your next stride without its rolling away from you. If you do not push it far enough, you will tend to trip over it, or you will have to break your running rhythm.

In the early stages, practice dribbling the ball along a straight line, varying the speed of your running and the type of dribble: e.g., use alternate feet, or only the outside of the foot, or four touches with the left foot, followed by four touches with the right.

Dribbling Exercise. Set up a line of obstacles about 6 feet apart (stones, sticks, soda cans—anything will do) and weave your way in and out of them with the ball, going to the left of the first obstacle, to the right of the second, and so on. Use the inside and the outside of both feet, keeping the ball under close control at all times. Every so often, time yourself on the run to see how much improvement you're making, and set up identical obstacle courses so that you can compare your dribbling skill with other players'.

Running with the Ball. When you have beaten an opponent by dribbling past him, or when you receive the ball in the clear, close control of the ball is no longer necessary. You must now make ground quickly, so push it farther ahead and run faster after it. Because it provides a more natural foot position for fast running, use the outside of the foot. You should use your favored foot, pushing the ball ahead so that you play it with each forward swing of that foot.

Dribbling Feints. To the three vital factors of close ball control, variation of pace and change of direction—you must now add body and foot feints to your dribbling skills.

It is quite common for the dribbler to find himself challenged by an opponent running alongside him, waiting for a chance to take the ball away. In this case, learn to play the ball only with the foot farthest away from the opponent: If he is running to your left, play the ball with your right foot, so that your left leg and your body are between him and the ball. If you can't outpace him, you must try to deceive him. Learn to stop suddenly in the middle of a dribble by placing your foot on top of the ball. If you can disguise your intention well enough, the opponent's momentum will carry him two or three paces past you before he reacts, giving you time to cut behind him or to pass to a teammate.

So you've deceived your opponent once by stopping suddenly. But next time he is going to be ready, he is going to be looking for that slightly higher lift of your leg necessary to get your foot on top of the ball—and that will be the ideal moment for him to move in. But you must be ready too. This time you don't stop the ball. You perform the feint shown in Figure 28.

A common method of getting around an opponent waiting in front of you is to fake a pass in one direction, then move the ball quickly in the opposite direction, as in Figure 29. Remember that, in any feint, you must convince your opponent that you propose to move or make a pass in a certain direction. Normally he will react to defend against that move, and precisely at that moment you must make your countermove. Experienced defenders can delay their reaction to your initial move so that they remain in a good position to do something about your countermove. Thus, you have to learn not only to make your own fakes convincing but also to recognize whether you have truly de-

A

Figure 28. Dribbling Feint—1

B

A. White is dribbling, under challenge from Black.

B. Black begins to move ahead, where he will be in a good position to challenge for the ball.

C. White lifts his right foot as though to stop the ball. Black starts to move in. But White does not stop the ball—instead he swings his foot back without touching the ball, while giving a little hop on his left foot to maintain his stride. (Note how playing the ball with the foot farthest away from the opponent makes it difficult for Black to get a clear view of it.)

D. White brings his right foot down behind ball and—without touching it to the ground—swings it forward into the ball, moving off quickly in his original direction, and leaving Black flat-footed.

C

D

Figure 29. Dribbling Feint—2

A. White is feinting to pass the ball. His head and body positions and leg action have convinced Black that the ball is going to his left, and he has committed himself to intercepting it, moving his left leg across. But at the last possible moment White curls his foot around the ball. He now has Black off balance and vulnerable, and can beat him in either of two ways:

A

ceived your opponent or whether he, in turn, is trying to fake you.

Back-heeling. Another method of deceiving a defender is to pass your foot forward over the ball and then kick it backward, using the heel, while making a short hop on the other foot. Before making a back-heel pass you must, of course,

56

B

B. By pushing the ball
through his legs.

C. By pulling the ball
back sharply and taking
it past Black's right side.

C

make certain that there is a teammate behind you ready to
receive the ball. Back-heeling can also be performed by
crossing one foot in front of the other: e.g., if you are

dribbling the ball with the outside of your right foot, cross your left foot over and swing it backward to hit the ball. While this method enables you to pass at an angle as well as directly backward, it is difficult to perform at speed because of the danger of tripping yourself as you make the move.

Screening. If you find your path blocked by an opponent whom you cannot fake out of position, you must try to retain possession and prevent him from getting at the ball. This is screening the ball—turning your body so that it is between him and the ball, as in Figure 30.

Figure 30. Screening
A. White has dribbled the ball in from the right and, unable to get past the defender Black, screens the ball by turning sideways.
B. By allowing Black to see the ball, but keeping it just out of his reach, White tempts him to move around into a position where he can challenge White for possession. Notice how White is looking in a direction that allows him to see both the ball and the opponent, and how his left leg is positioned and bent at the knee, making it difficult for Black to get at the ball.

C and D. If Black makes a move to get to the ball, White can suddenly accelerate his turn, spinning away to his right, using the outside of his right foot to move the ball away.

TACKLING

In soccer, "tackling" means using your feet to take the ball from the feet of an opponent. You are not allowed to grab hold of your opponent or push him or block him or use any of the methods that are legitimate in football. You must not trip him; nor can you jump in with both feet. Despite these restrictions, it is usually the tackler who wins tackles because all he is trying to do is to block the ball, he is not trying to dribble it past his opponent, as is the player in possession.

Defensive Stance. As a defender preparing to tackle, take up the stance shown in Figure 31. Determination and timing are what count in tackling. Be sure to plant your tackling foot firmly on the ground to block the ball before your opponent can play it away. And you must be prepared for some body contact—it may be your knee or thigh or chest or shoulder.

Figure 31. Defensive Stance
Stand on your toes, ready to move in any direction, to spin on the ball of your foot if you have to turn quickly. Crouching forward slightly gives you a more stable position, so that you are not likely to be knocked off balance making your tackle.

Front Block Tackle. In tackling from the front, your aim should be to get solidly behind the ball and block it—do not try to kick it away. The technique is shown in Figure 32. Try not to be caught with your legs spread out. Position them as in Figure 32B: far enough apart for good balance, but not so far apart that the ball can slip between them.

Figure 32. Front Block Tackle
A. Defender Black is moving in to take the ball from White.

A

B. White tries to avoid the tackle by moving the ball to his left. Black gets his right foot behind the ball to block this move.

C. Black now transfers his weight to his right foot and has the ball solidly blocked. White's attempt to move to his left is causing him to spin away, off balance, leaving Black in possession of the ball.

B   C

A

Figure 33. Sliding Tackle
A. Defender Black is running across to intercept White.

Sliding Tackle. This demonstrates one of the greatest assets that a defender can have: the ability to reach, to stretch an extra inch or two for the ball. The defender is usually running across the field to cut off an attacker who has broken through on his own. Thus the sliding tackle is often used in desperation situations, and the aim is to kick the ball away from the attacker, not to gain possession. If you can kick the ball away so that it goes to a teammate, that is a bonus. Figure 33 illustrates the approach and kick. The tackle must be perfectly timed because of the risk of missing the ball and perhaps tripping the attacker—which will mean a foul and a free kick against you. If you play the ball away first, before making contact with your opponent, there will be no foul. It is then up to the attacker to avoid your legs. And remember that after a sliding tackle, you will be sitting on the ground. If you have only tipped the ball away lightly, the attacker will regather it and you will not be able to do anything to stop him. Kick the ball solidly— to a teammate if you can, out of bounds if you cannot.

B. Black, preparing to reach out with his right foot, must time his tackle so that he makes contact with the ball before White can play it again.

C. Going down on his left side while breaking his fall with his left hand, Black slides his right foot forward to kick the ball solidly away. Here he has hit the ball with his instep—but it could have been with his toe. This is one of the rare instances in soccer when the toe may be used to advantage—it provides an extra inch or two of reach.

Sliding Block Tackle. Clearly, if you *can* get possession of the ball when tackling, you should—and by using the sliding block tackle, you can. Only your own judgment and experience will tell you when to use this tackle rather than the straight sliding tackle, but for the block tackle you obviously need a fraction more time. The approach for the two tackles is the same; Figure 34 shows the blocking action.

Figure 34. Sliding Block Tackle
A. Defender Black slides in on his left side, with the right foot raised, ready to hook it around the ball rather than kick it away.
B. Ball is firmly blocked by Black. White's forward momentum will carry him a step or two farther on, giving Black time to regain his feet, with the ball under control.

Figure 35. Shoulder Charging
Arms must be kept close to the side to avoid illegal use of elbows, and the ball must be within playing distance. Black is moving in to dispossess White. White has braced for the contact by leaning slightly toward his opponent.

Shoulder Charging. This is the one form of body contact that the soccer rules allow. The aim is to nudge or barge your opponent away from the ball by making solid contact with your shoulder against his (see Figure 35). You must not charge him in the back and you must not use your elbows or hips. Remember: your aim is to win possession of the ball—you are not trying to knock your opponent into the next field. If, in a game, the referee considers your charging too violent or dangerous, he will give a free kick against you.

PRACTICING

We have now dealt with all the fundamental ball skills. From here on it is up to you to perfect them. Practice as often as you can, dividing your time equally between:

1. Ball control exercise: keeping the ball airborne, using your feet, thighs, chest and head.

2. Playing the ball off the wall: by kicking, volleying and heading. Increase the speed of the exercise by moving closer to the wall.

3. Dribbling and running with the ball.

4
Goalkeeping

AS the only player allowed to use his hands, the goalkeeper must develop a unique set of skills, quite different from those of other soccer players. He needs, above all, agility and a safe pair of hands.

THE GOALKEEPER'S BALL SKILLS

The Golden Rule of goalkeeping is: Get your body behind the ball whenever possible, and clasp it securely to your chest as you catch it (see Figure 36).

Ground Balls. Shots coming straight at you along the ground may appear to be easy to deal with, but do not handle them casually. There is always the chance of the ball taking an unexpected bounce, so get down on one knee, as in Figure 37.

High Balls. For high balls—those coming in above your head—the rule is to catch them as soon as you can. Do not

Figure 36. Saving a Chest-High-Shot
Lean slightly forward so that the force of the shot will not push you backward, off balance, as you grasp the ball tightly to your chest. Some goalkeepers like to wear goalkeeping gloves, particularly on wet days, but the majority will not do so under normal, dry, conditions.

A

Figure 37. Gathering a Ground Ball
A. Position your body at a slight angle to the path of the ball with one knee on the ground, the other pointing across the path of the ball, so that your hands are backed up by your legs. Make sure you do not leave a gap through which the ball could squeeze if you mishandle it.

B. Gather the ball out in front of you and immediately let it roll up your forearms and clasp it to your chest. Get to your feet in the position shown in Figure 36 (page 69), so that you are prepared to avoid or withstand a collision with an opponent without going over the line into your goal. (The position of your feet does not matter, but if you carry the ball over the line, it is a goal for your opponents.)

B

stand around waiting for them to come to you. Go to meet them, and when other players are around, this means that you will usually have to jump for them. Practice timing your jumps so that, with your arms fully stretched above you, you can collect the ball at the highest point of your leap, as in Figure 38.

Figure 38. High Balls
Always try to face the flight of the ball and place your hands slightly to the back of the ball. Raising your knee slightly as a protective measure to keep away opponents who may run into you, catch the ball, bring it down and clasp it to your chest in one movement.

Punching and Deflecting. There will always be those balls that your judgment tells you are going to be difficult to catch—either they are too high or they are going too fast or perhaps there are too many opponents around you. Such balls must be cleared from the goal mouth as quickly as possible. One method is to punch them away. If you can get

70

both clenched fists, held side by side, onto the ball, so much the better; but in any case, whether using two hands or one, punch with power. Try to hit the ball as far away as you can. Avoid punching across the flight of the ball— either hit it back in the direction from which it came or, if it is going across the goal, help it on its way.

Another method of removing danger from high balls is to deflect them round the post or over the bar. The most dangerous are those coming in at about the height of the crossbar. These should be swept over the bar (Figure 39).

**Figure 39. Tipping Ball
Over Crossbar**
Tip the ball over the bar with the palm of the hand or the fingertips, using a slightly upward pushing motion. Make certain that the ball **does** go over the bar—a too casual approach could lead to your pushing the ball onto the face of the crossbar so that it bounces back into play.

Punching and deflecting, essential as they are to the goalkeeper's skill, should be used only when you are not certain that you can hold on to the ball.

Diving Saves. The most spectacular of the goalie's moves—and the ones that always excite the fans—are the diving saves. For these you need a combination of agility, power-

Figure 40. Diving Save

A

A. As soon as you have caught the ball, move your arms downward, so that—

ful leg thrust, safe ball handling and confidence that you can land without hurting yourself. Practice diving to the side, without the ball, kicking your legs upward to make sure that when you land a part of your upper body—hands, arms or shoulders—touches the ground first. Most goalkeepers prefer to get the ball to the ground as soon as possible after catching it, and they use the technique shown in Figure 40. With diving saves, as with all other saves, if you are not completely confident of holding onto the ball, punch it away or deflect it wide of the goal.

72

B.—the forearm and the ball are first to make contact with the ground, while the upper hand pushes the ball down.

C. As soon as you can, pull the ball into your chest to prevent its rolling loose at the feet of opponents who may be waiting nearby for just such a slip.

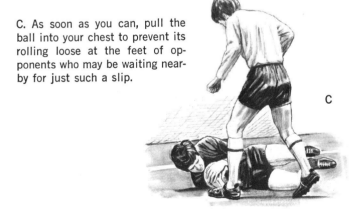

Diving for Ground Balls. Ground balls coming in fast and wide of you must also be clasped to your chest, which means getting your trunk on to the ground as quickly as possible. Do not throw your legs up, but make a diving fall so that your knee or thigh touches the ground first, as in Figure 41A.

Figure 41. Diving for Ground Balls
A. When diving onto a ground ball, get your body down as quickly as possible—the danger is that a fast-moving ball will slip under your body.

A

B. Clutch the ball and draw it into your chest. If an opponent is challenging, you can protect the ball—and yourself—by rolling over so that your forearm and shoulder are shielding the ball. But this position does allow a greater chance of the ball squeezing loose beyond you. The position shown in 40C (page 73) is certainly safer when no opponent is challenging.

B

Distribution. As a goalkeeper it is clearly understood that you are the last line of defense, but it is often less clearly realized that you are also the player who starts many attacking moves. Distribution is, simply, what you do with the ball after you have gained possession. It is up to you to throw it or roll it to a well-placed teammate. Often it is an advantage for you to get rid of the ball quickly, stopping the opponents' attack and starting one of your own all in the same movement, in which case you should use the throw shown in Figure 42. However, if you cannot spot an unmarked colleague, then punt the ball for distance—punts of 50 or 60 yards are common in top-class soccer.

Figure 42. Goalkeeper Throwing Ball
The action of the goalkeeper's throw is that of a side-arm baseball pitcher. Hold your hand at the back of, and slightly underneath, the ball. Throw the ball hard and low to avoid interception; don't try to lob it unless you have to throw it over the head of a player to reach a teammate.

Positioning. Next to a safe pair of hands, the goalie's most vital asset is knowing how to position himself correctly, how to move into the right spot as, or preferably *before*, the shot is made. If you can do this, you will cut down the number of desperation saves and last-second moves that you have to make, and greatly reduce the risk of error. Remember: your errors are likely to be fatal because there is often only the open goal behind you. Great goalkeepers develop the art of positioning to an almost uncanny degree so that shots seem always to come straight at them and they have to do a minimum of diving and leaping. "Making it look easy" is the hallmark of a good goalkeeper, so do not assume that a goalie who is constantly and acrobatically diving is great—maybe his positional play is at fault.

Your basic position should be the center of the goal, about 1 yard in front of the goal line, but you must be prepared to run out to gather low or high balls—certainly within a 6- or 8-yard range, and often up to 15 yards. If a ball is coming in that you are confident of gathering before an opponent can get to it, then go for it. But let your teammates—who will usually have their backs to you—know you are coming. Shout loudly and decisively for the ball.

In fact, as the goalkeeper, you should be a commanding presence in the penalty area, shouting to your teammates where to position themselves. If you show good judgment with your calls, they will obey you because you, being behind them, are the only one who can see most of what is going on. Clever guidance of your defenders' positions and play can greatly limit the shooting opportunities for opposing forwards—another way of making things easier for yourself! And when you shout, do so loudly and with authority. A silent or indecisive goalkeeper creates enormous problems for defenders relying on him for guidance.

Advancing from Goal. On those occasions when an opponent has broken clear of your defenders and is racing

76

unchallenged toward your goal, you *must* run out toward him. This is a matter of simple geometry, known as narrowing the angle, and is explained in Diagram 2.

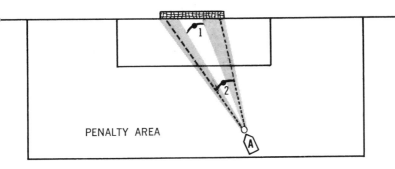

Diagram 2. Narrowing the Angle
If goalkeeper stays on his line at Position 1, he leaves large areas of open goal (shaded) on both sides of him, and he allows the Attacker A to close in. But if the goalkeeper comes out to Position 2, he makes the attacker shoot from farther out and considerably reduces the area of goal at which he can aim (the shaded area **outside** the dotted lines). In this position the goalkeeper has only to divert the ball slightly to send it wide of the goal.

When you do advance from your goal line, beware of the ball being lobbed or chipped over your head. There is not too much danger of this if the opponent is running toward you with the ball on the ground (because of the difficulty an attacker will have in chipping a ball rolling away from him) but if the ball is bouncing in front of him, be on guard. If he gets it over your head, your only hope will be that it also goes over the goal.

You have to learn when, and how far, and at what angle, to come out of your goal, and you have to be aware of the exact position of the goal behind you. To provide guides to your position relative to the goal, make three marks on the 6-yard line by scuffing it with your shoes: one opposite each goal post and one opposite the middle of the goal. By glancing at these marks as you advance you will learn to come out at precisely the angle that will make it most difficult for an attacker to score.

5
The Skills
in Action

TO be a soccer player you must master the skills we have been describing—but don't go off with the idea that that's all there is to it. Ball skills are simply the tools of the trade to be *used* in games where you will be playing alongside and against other players. During a normal eleven-a-side game you will probably have possession of the ball only about 5 per cent of the time, and you now have to start thinking about what you do during the remaining 95 per cent. You have to consider, not just your own actions, but those of your teammates and those of your opponents. In short, you have to be able to analyze game situations.

ANALYZING THE GAME

Whether you are involved as a player or watching as a spectator, you should build your analysis of soccer around three factors: Space, Time and Support. They are the keys to understanding the game of soccer and to assessing the all-round skill of individual players and teams. These are the sort of questions you should ask yourself:

Space: How much space do you need to perform your ball skills? If you are denied sufficient space by close guarding, can you create it by deceiving your opponent? Can you create space for your teammates by drawing opponents out of position? If you are a defender, how tightly are you marking your opponent—which means simply: How much space are you allowing him?

Time: How much time do you need to perform your skills? (This is partly a matter of ball skill—the less skilled will require more time and space—and partly a matter of the speed with which a player makes decisions. Soccer is a game of constant analysis and instant decision-making, and 50 per cent of making the right decision is a matter of timing. What was the right decision 2 seconds ago may be the wrong one now. Timing is absolutely crucial when passing the ball.) Do you pass only when *you* are ready to pass? Or are you also aware of your teammates' moves and problems so that you pass when they are best positioned to receive?

Support: When you do not have the ball, are you doing everything you can for your teammates? Are you always aware of their problems? Do you help them by shouting instructions or by taking up positions where you can receive the ball? (The more support a player with the ball has, the greater the number of alternative moves that he can make. Similarly, from a defender's point of view, it is comforting to know that other defenders are around, shouting advice or directions, and ready to cover any errors.)

SMALL-TEAM GAMES

Space, Time, Support—put them all together and they add up to Teamwork. It is the purpose of this section to introduce you to skills you must develop when playing with and against other players—skills that are best learned in small-team games. To plunge straight into a full 11-a-side team game is perhaps enjoyable, but not quite as beneficial at this stage: young players in particular tend to be overwhelmed by the amount of space and the twenty-one other players. It is far better to restrict your playing to a small but definite area and to limit the number of players. You will never perfect your skills if you are allowed to chase the ball into the next field to control it or to avoid close guarding.

Because of the importance of space and the necessity of boundaries for these games, it is strongly recommended that you mark off a 20-yard square into four areas of 10 yards square. This will allow you to use the area that your skill justifies, and the over-all size is large enough to accommodate four- or five-a-side team games.

In all small-team games it is also essential to have some method of scoring. You may set up a can that has to be knocked down with the ball, or two sticks between which the ball has to roll on the ground; or it may be that a team has to retain possession of the ball for a certain time, or has to make a fixed number of consecutive passes.

But above all, in these games, develop that habit of constantly analyzing the situation, of carrying on a continuous question-and-answer conversation with yourself. Think in terms of: "How can I become a better player?" rather than: "Well, I'm a better player than So-and-So anyway!"

Two-Against-One: The Wall Pass—1. (Area: 10 yards square.) The simplest example of teamwork is a two-against-one situation, which gives an attacking player the opportunity either to dribble past the defender or to beat him by exchanging passes with a supporting attacker. The two-pass movement—soccer's version of the give-and-go—is called the wall pass because in street-corner soccer the ball is usually bounced off a wall rather than passed to a teammate.

The wall-pass situation (see Diagram 3) contains many of the basic problems that soccer players have to be able to solve. Imagine yourself in the role of each player in turn:

Attacker A: How should I approach the defender—by running straight at him or at an angle? At full or reduced

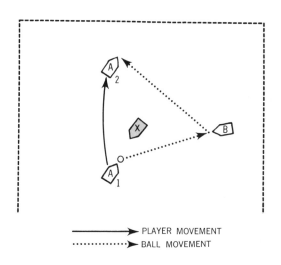

PLAYER MOVEMENT
BALL MOVEMENT

Diagram 3. The Wall Pass
A dribbles the ball toward Defender X until, at position A_1, he passes it along the ground to B. B plays it first time, behind the Defender X, as A sprints to the left of X to receive the return pass at position A_2.

speed? How close to him can I safely take the ball? At the same time that I am watching the defender, am I also aware of the movements of my supporting player B? If, at the very last moment, I see that the defender is positioned to intercept my pass, can I hold back the pass? (You will find that you should go straight at the defender at a fairly fast pace, giving yourself two alternatives: to pass or to dribble past him at the last second. If you are prepared to pass the ball with the outside of the foot nearest your supporting player, you can go to within 3 feet of the defender, giving yourself a much better chance to sprint into the clear to receive the return pass.)

Defender X: How close can I allow A to come before moving in to tackle him? Am I aware of exactly where B is positioned? Can I take up a position that will block A's direct run at goal and, at the same time, prevent him from passing to B? Can I, by faking to tackle, force A to pass when I want him to, when I know that I have good position and can intercept?

Attacker B: Am I at the right angle to receive the pass? (Too deep, and A will be unable to make the first pass, too shallow and I shall not be able to make the return pass.) Am I aware of X's movements *after* A has made the first pass? If X has moved into a position to block the return pass, can I decide quickly enough *not* to pass?

Three-or-Four-Against-One. Still using the same 10-yard-square area, increase the number of attackers to three or four, with the lone defender as the man in the middle. He must try to intercept the ball while the others interpass it. He does not have to control it; just getting a foot to it is enough. When he does so, or when the ball goes out of the area, the player who made the error goes into the middle. By making this a one-touch game—meaning that the attackers must play the ball away first time with only one kick—you will learn how important it is to *pace* your passes properly and to conceal their direction until the last possible moment. If you hit them too hard, your teammates will have difficulty playing them away without controlling them first and will have no time to be deceptive. If you hit them too softly, the defender will have time to intercept them.

Two-Against-Two: The Wall Pass—2. (Area: 10 yards square.) The addition of an extra defender, Y, makes the wall pass much more difficult to complete. Attacker A must now learn the art of passing to a marked man, placing the ball always so that B can get to it while screening out Defender Y with his body. Attacker B must try to deceive Y with fake starts and runs but still be prepared to receive the ball from A at any time. He must also take note of the positions of all the other players the instant before the pass arrives. This is a vital rule for all players receiving the ball: Look *before* the pass arrives—you may not have time to look once you have the ball.

Defender Y must support X as he tries to win possession of the ball. He must decide whether to try to intercept the pass from A to B, or to tackle B as the ball arrives, or to wait and try to intercept the return pass to A. He must shout advice on positioning to X, and be prepared to receive advice in return. The attacking pair, A and B, should also be shouting advice to each other.

In two-against-two games, the roles of attackers and defenders are constantly changing as possession is won and lost. Learning to adapt instantly from offensive to defensive thinking and positioning, and vice versa, is a crucial part of soccer.

Three-Against-Two. (Area: 15–20 yards square.) With three attackers, a new factor is introduced: Attacker A now has to follow the moves of two supporting players B and C and decide which one he should pass to. Each supporting player must be constantly assessing the positions of all the players and be ready to move into a better position to help Attacker A or to draw a defender away from the other supporting player. This unselfish off-the-ball running, or decoy running, is vital to make sure that one defender cannot mark two attackers. For each defender the problem is one of positioning: where to place himself so that if possible he can cover two attackers at the same time. This type of off-the-ball running and defensive positioning is illustrated in Diagram 4. Each pass brings an entirely new set of circumstances to be analyzed and requires constant movement of players into appropriate supporting positions.

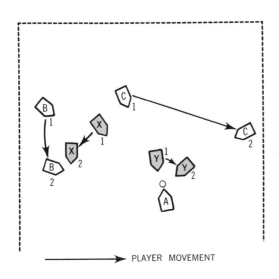

PLAYER MOVEMENT

Diagram 4. Three-Against-Two

Initially, Defender X_1 is in a good position to intercept any pass from A to B_1 or C_1. However, as B_1 moves to position B_2, Defender X_1 must move to X_2 to prevent an obvious pass from A to B_2. At this point Defender Y_1 is in a good position to tackle player A, and he can also intercept any pass intended for C_1. Realizing that he is in a poor supporting position, C_1 moves to C_2. At the same time, Defender X should be advising Y_1 that C is moving behind him into another position, and he should be talking Y_1 into position Y_2 to prevent a pass reaching C_2.

Three-Against-Three. (Area: 20 yards square.) Games involving three players per team provide the ideal opportunity to develop all-round defensive and offensive skill. The larger area makes it practical to use goalkeepers. You can either have the goalkeepers in goal all the time, leaving the remaining players to play two-against-two, or make a rule that whichever team is defending must position one of its players in goal, while the team in possession attacks with three players. When possession of the ball changes, the goalkeeper comes out and the other team must withdraw one of its players to play in goal. Give him time to take up his position by ruling that attacks can only begin with the ball in the goalkeeper's hands, either as the result of a save, a goal kick or a pass back by one of his two defenders.

Vary the rules for all these small-team games so that you increase their competitiveness or accent some particular skill of the sport—e.g., allow only two touches, or one touch, of the ball to each player; allow only left-foot or right-foot kicking.

HEADING GAMES

To develop your skill at heading, three-against-three or four-against-four games of Throw-Head-Catch are ideal. The ball is thrown (with the hands!) to a teammate, who *must* head it. He tries to head it to a teammate, who catches the ball (with his hands!). He cannot run or walk while holding the ball, but must make another throwing pass, which must be headed. If the opposing team intercepts, it must do so in the throw-head-catch sequence. It cannot intercept a throw by catching the ball, but only by heading it.

Another excellent practice game is heading tennis, played on a regular tennis court with three or four players on each side. After crossing the net, the ball is allowed to bounce once only, after which players must keep it in the air using feet, thighs, chest or head. It can be passed from player to player on the same side, after which it must be played back across the net by heading it.

INDOOR SOCCER

Finally, there is indoor soccer, played with five, six or seven players on a team, depending on the area available, with reduced-size goals of 5 yards by 5 feet or even smaller. School gymnasiums are ideal for this, and regular practice on a good surface, rebounding the ball off the wall wherever possible, will sharpen your game in preparing you for the wide-open spaces of a regular soccer field.

TEAM FORMATIONS

This is a subject in itself, as extensive as in football or hockey or basketball. There have been, during soccer's long history, countless ways of deploying the eleven players, with the goalkeeper's position probably the only one that hasn't changed its function to any major extent.

A **Diagram 5. Team Formations** B

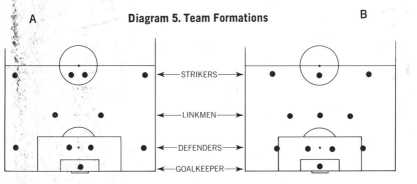

A. 4–2–4 Formation.   B. 4–3–3 Formation.

For players learning the game the best of the modern formations is the 4–2–4 (Diagram 5A). This means 4 defenders, 2 linkmen and 4 strikers. Soccer formations always start at the back and work forward; the goalkeeper is never included, since his position never varies. The 4–2–4 is a balanced formation, giving an equal spread of players over the playing area and an equal division between defense and attack. Another, more defensive-minded formation that is much in use is the 4–3–3 (Diagram 5B); but for young players—where emphasis should be on the development of all-round skill—such a formation is too defense-oriented.

As in most team sports the formation a team adopts is simply a general outline of playing methods. Within that formation there must be freedom for players to use their initiative by interchanging positions when the opportunity arises.

POSITIONS

Let us take a closer look at the four types of soccer player: goalkeepers, defenders, linkmen and strikers. We have talked about goalkeepers (see pages 68–79), and they are the only players who have to develop unique skills. The other players require an all-round ability with certain specialized skills.

Defenders (Backs). These players should be strong tacklers, capable of making powerful clearances and confident at heading high balls powerfully and accurately. They must be able to concentrate on guarding their opponents rather than following the ball. (Defenders who are ball watchers allow their opponents to sneak into better attacking positions.) They should be skillful at anticipating attacking moves so that they are quick to intercept passes.

90

Linkmen (Midfielders). These are the "engine room" of the team. They must be able to do everything, for they are both attackers and defenders. They must have exceptional stamina. Great players in this position are often rather small but aggressive in their desire to win the ball and shrewd with their passes in setting up opportunities to score. Changes in possession of the ball continually occur in midfield, and linkmen must therefore develop a sixth sense to anticipate each change. A numerical advantage in attack or defense can be created by the linkman who anticipates a change of possession.

Strikers (Forwards). These players must be able to cope with the attention of quick-tackling defenders. Their ball control, passing accuracy and particularly their skill at screening must be exceptional. Speed off the mark is a tremendous asset. *Central strikers* must be powerful and accurate in their shooting (with both feet) and their heading. *Wingers* must be able to beat defenders using speed, dribbling skills and wall passes with supporting players. Their passing must be accurate, and skill at chipping the ball to attackers in the goal mouth is vital.

THE GREAT PLAYER

The range of soccer skills is almost bewildering in its variety, and probably no one player can perfect them all or consistently apply them to advantage. Yet there are certain key skills that seem to distinguish the truly great players:

- Total mastery of heading, volleying and chipping, and of pacing and timing passes correctly.
- Ability to control and screen the ball when harassed by an opponent.
- Keen sense of anticipation, which indicates a total awareness of the positions of all players at all times.

91

- Ability to change direction and pace suddenly and to deceive opponents as to intentions.
- Being willing, and knowing when, to take opponents out of position to create an opening for a teammate.
- Poise and composure, built on confidence that his superior ball skills and total awareness will enable him to deal with any situation.
- Strength of character and leadership that makes it natural to accept responsibility even when the remainder of the team are having a difficult time.

For many, the chief characteristic of a great player is skill in retaining possession in spite of successive tackles by opponents. For others, the most important asset is the ability to play the ball away accurately to a teammate with a first-time pass even when under pressure from one or more opponents. It indicates not only that the player has developed a keen sense of touch with all his ball skills but also that he knows—before he receives the ball—exactly where teammates and opponents are positioned.

It has been the aim of this book, first, to develop your individual skill in all the basic soccer techniques, second, to give you a clear, analytical way of thinking about soccer as a team sport and, third, to combine these two—the physical and the mental—into the over-all skills that will make you a rounded soccer player. If you can absorb, practice and perfect everything you have read, then eleven-a-side soccer will hold no fears for you. You will be a player whom any coach will welcome to his team.